W9-APK-533

CREATION

"In the beginning God created the heaven and the earth."

—Genesis 1:1
The Holy Bible

God Created Me And Everything Else That Exists. There Is No Other God.

2

FAITH

"But without faith it is impossible to please Him: for he that cometh to God must believe that He is, and that He is a rewarder of them that diligently seek Him."

—Hebrews 11:6

The Holy Bible

My Obedience To The Law Of God Gives Me Confidence That He Will Answer Any Prayers.

3

FEAR OF GOD

"The fear of the Lord is the beginning of wisdom:"

–Proverbs 9:10
The Holy Bible

My Respect For God Shows I Have Wisdom.

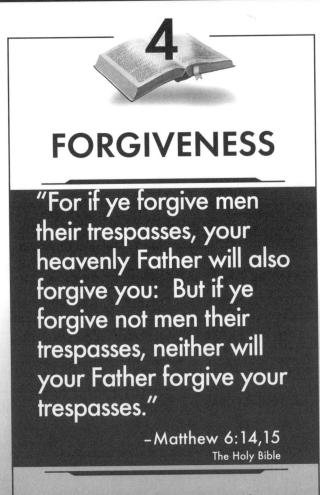

4

FORGIVENESS

"For if ye forgive men their trespasses, your heavenly Father will also forgive you: But if ye forgive not men their trespasses, neither will your Father forgive your trespasses."

–Matthew 6:14,15
The Holy Bible

When I Forgive Others, God Forgives Me.

5

GOD

"Acquaint now thyself with Him, and be at peace: thereby good shall come unto thee."

–Job 22:21
The Holy Bible

God Is My Best Friend And Makes Good Things Happen For My Life.

HEAVEN

"I go to prepare a place for you."

-John 14:2
The Holy Bible

Jesus Returned To Heaven To Prepare An Eternal Home For Me.

HOLY SPIRIT

"And I will pray the Father, and He shall give you another Comforter, that He may abide with you for ever;"

–John 14:16
The Holy Bible

The Holy Spirit Is My Present Invisible Teacher Who Walks Beside Me Daily.

- 7 -

8

JESUS

"Jesus said unto her, I am the resurrection, and the life: he that believeth in Me, though he were dead, yet shall he live:"

–John 11:25
The Holy Bible

Jesus Rose From The Dead And Is Coming Back To Earth Again.

9

JOY

"Thou wilt shew me
the path of life: in
Thy presence is
fulness of joy; at Thy
right hand there are
pleasures for
evermore."

—Psalm 16:11
The Holy Bible

*God Will Always Show Me The Path I
Should Walk In Life. His Joy Within Me
Will Be The Proof Of His Presence With Me.*

10

LOVE

"By this shall all men know that ye are My disciples, if ye have love one to another."

–John 13:35
The Holy Bible

My Love For Others Is The Evidence To Others That Jesus Lives Within Me.

11

MEMORIZING
THE BIBLE

"The law of his God is in his heart; none of his steps shall slide."

–Psalm 37:31
The Holy Bible

The More I Memorize The Word Of God, The Stronger And Wiser I Become.

12

MISTAKES

"If we confess our sins, He is faithful and just to forgive us our sins, and to cleanse us from all unrighteousness."

– 1 John 1:9
The Holy Bible

When I Do Wrong, God Will Forgive Me When I Repent.

13

PARENTS

"Honor thy father and mother; which is the first commandment with promise; That it may be well with thee, and thou mayest live long on the earth."

–Ephesians 6:2,3
The Holy Bible

When I Honor And Obey My Parents, God Blesses Me.

14

PEACE

"Great peace have they which love Thy law: and nothing shall offend them."

-Psalm 119:165
The Holy Bible

When I Do Right, I Feel Real Peaceful Inside.

15

POWER

"But ye shall receive power, after that the Holy Ghost is come upon you: and ye shall be witnesses unto Me both in Jerusalem, and in all Judaea, and in Samaria, and unto the uttermost part of the earth."

–Acts 1:8
The Holy Bible

I Have The Power To Do Right Because The Holy Spirit Lives Inside Me.

16

PRAISE

"Enter into His gates with thanksgiving, and into His courts with praise: be thankful unto Him and bless His name."

–Psalm 100:4
The Holy Bible

When I Sing And Worship God, He Surrounds Me With His Presence.

17

PRAYER

"And all things, whatsoever ye shall ask in prayer, believing, ye shall receive."

–Matthew 21:22
The Holy Bible

I Always Expect God To Answer My Prayers Because I Believe His Word.

18

PROSPERITY

"And it shall come to pass, if thou shalt hearken diligently unto the voice of the Lord thy God, to observe and to do all His commandments which I command thee this day, that the Lord thy God will set thee on high above all nations of the earth: And all these blessings shall come on thee, and overtake thee, if thou shalt hearken unto the voice of the Lord thy God."

–Deuteronomy 28:1,2
The Holy Bible

I Always Obey God And He Rewards Me By Blessing Me Every Day.

19

PROTECTION

"The Lord is on my side; I will not fear: what can man do unto me?"

–Psalm 118:6
The Holy Bible

I Am Not Afraid Of Anything Because God Is Always Protecting Me.

20

SALVATION

"For God so loved the world, that He gave His only begotten Son, that whosoever believeth in Him should not perish, but have everlasting life."

–John 3:16
The Holy Bible

God Loved Me So Much He Gave His Son Jesus As His Special Gift.

21

SEED-FAITH

"Give, and it shall be given unto you; good measure, pressed down, and shaken together, and running over, shall men give into your bosom. For with the same measure that ye mete withal it shall be measured to you again."

–Luke 6:38
The Holy Bible

When I Give Something Special To God, It Is Like A Seed That Grows A Good Harvest Back For Me.

- 21 -

STUDYING

"Study to shew thyself approved unto God, a workman that needeth not to be ashamed, rightly dividing the word of truth."

–2 Timothy 2:15
The Holy Bible

I Study The Word Of God So I Can Know What He Wants Me To Do.

23

SUCCESS

"I can do all things through Christ which strengtheneth me."

–Philippians 4:13
The Holy Bible

I Can Achieve My Greatest Goals Because Jesus Lives Inside Me.

24

TEMPTATION

"There hath no temptation taken you but such as is common to man: but God is faithful, Who will not suffer you to be tempted above that ye are able; but will with the temptation also make a way to escape, that ye may be able to bear it."

–1 Corinthians 10:13
The Holy Bible

When I Am Tempted To Do Wrong, God Will Always Give Me The Power To Just Say No.

25

THANKFULNESS

"In every thing give thanks: for this is the will of God in Christ Jesus concerning you."

–1 Thessalonians 5:18

The Holy Bible

I Will Constantly Show My Thankfulness To God Because This Brings Him Joy.

- 25 -

26

THE SECRET PLACE

"He that dwelleth in The Secret Place of the most High shall abide under the shadow of the Almighty."

–Psalm 91:1
The Holy Bible

The Secret Place Is The Special Place Where I Talk To God Every Morning.

27

THOUGHTS

"For as he thinketh in his heart, so is he:"

–Proverbs 23:7
The Holy Bible

My Thoughts Are Very Powerful, That Is Why I Think About The Goodness Of God All The Time Because What I Think About Will Keep Happening In My Life.

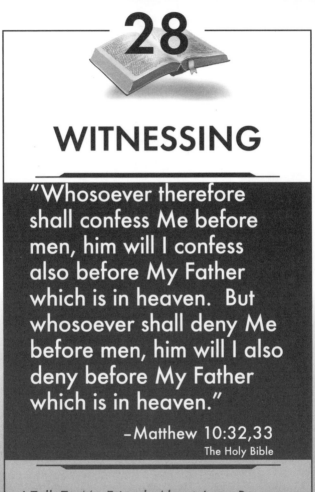

28

WITNESSING

"Whosoever therefore shall confess Me before men, him will I confess also before My Father which is in heaven. But whosoever shall deny Me before men, him will I also deny before My Father which is in heaven."

–Matthew 10:32,33
The Holy Bible

I Talk To My Friends About Jesus Because I Want Them To Love Him Too.

29

WORD OF GOD

"Thy word is a lamp unto my feet, and a light unto my path."

–Psalm 119:105
The Holy Bible

The Word Of God Helps Me Make Good Decisions During The Difficult Times Of My Life.

- 29 -

30

WORDS

"Pleasant words are as an honeycomb, sweet to the soul, and health to the bones."

–Proverbs 16:24
The Holy Bible

I Will Always Speak Happy And Encouraging Words To Others. When I Do, I Feel Happy And Good Inside.

31

WISDOM

"Wisdom is the principal thing; therefore get wisdom: and with all thy getting get understanding."

—Proverbs 4:7
The Holy Bible

Wisdom Is The Scriptural Answer To Any Problem I Face. That Is Why The Wisdom Of God Is The Most Important Thing In My Life.

- 31 -

DECISION

Do You Want Jesus To Be The King Of Your Life And Ruler Of Your Heart?

God's Book, the Bible says, "For God so loved the world, that He gave His only begotten Son that whosoever believeth in Him should not perish, but have everlasting life" (John 3:16). Jesus loves you very much and wants to help you be the best person you can be. But, it is your choice if you want Jesus to be the King of your life.

To make Jesus the King of your life all you have to do is talk to Jesus by praying the following prayer: *"Dear Jesus, I ask You to come into my life today, and to forgive me for anything I have done that was not good. I believe that You died for me and that you will forgive me when I do wrong things. Thank You for Your love and forgiveness. I love you, Jesus, and I accept you now as the King of my life and the Ruler of my heart. In Jesus' name. Amen."*

Remember to talk to Jesus every day. Tell Him that you love Him and anything else you want Him to know. Always remember how much Jesus loves you!

☐ Yes, Mike! I prayed to Jesus today and ask Him to be the King of my life. Please send me my free gift of your book *"31 Keys to a New Beginning"* to help me with my new life in Christ. *(B-48)*

Name _____ Birthdate ___ / ___

Address _____

City _____ State _____ Zip _____

Phone (___) _____ E-Mail _____

(B-140)

Mail To:
The Wisdom Center · P.O. Box 99 · Denton, TX 76202
1-888-WISDOM-1 (1-888-947-3661)
Website: www.thewisdomcenter.tv

Unless otherwise indicated, all Scripture quotations are taken from the King James Version of the Bible.
31 Scriptures Every Child Should Memorize · ISBN 1-56394-172-4/B-140
Copyright © 2002 by MIKE MURDOCK
All publishing rights belong exclusively to Wisdom International
Published by The Wisdom Center · P. O. Box 99 • Denton, Texas 76202
1-888-WISDOM-1 (1-888-947-3661) · Website: www.thewisdomcenter.tv
Printed in the United States of America. All rights reserved under International Copyright Law. Contents and/or cover may not be reproduced in whole or in part in any form without the express written consent of the Publisher. 01-030-10K

UNCOMMON WISDOM FOR UNCOMMON POWER

THE *Power* 7

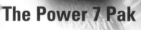

The Power 7 Pak

Seeds of Wisdom on The Secret Place (B-115 / $5)
Seeds of Wisdom on The Holy Spirit (B-116 / $5)
Seeds of Wisdom on Your Assignment (B-122 / $5)
Seeds of Wisdom on Goal Setting (B-127 / $5)
My Personal Dream Book (B-143 / $5)
101 Wisdom Keys (B-45 / $5)
31 Keys To A New Beginning (B-48 / $5)

The Wisdom Center
All 7 Books
Only $20
WBL-19
Wisdom Is The Principal Thing

Add 10% For S/H

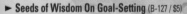

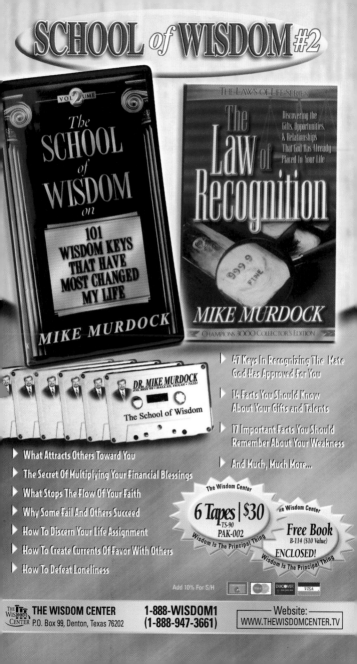

Songs From The Secret Place!

The Music Ministry of **MIKE MURDOCK**

SONGS FROM THE SECRET PLACE

Love Songs To The Holy Spirit Birthed In The Secret Place

THE HOLY SPIRIT HANDBOOK

What You Need To Know About Your Daily Companion, The Holy Spirit

Volume 1

MIKE MURDOCK

The Wisdom Center

6 Tapes | $30
TS-59
PAK-007

Wisdom Is The Principal Thing

Free Book
B-100 ($10 Value)
ENCLOSED!

Wisdom Is The Principal Thing

Songs...

1. A Holy Place
2. Anything You Want
3. Everything Comes From You
4. Fill This Place With Your Presence
5. First Thing Every Morning
6. Holy Spirit, I Want To Hear You
7. Holy Spirit, Move Again
8. Holy Spirit, You Are Enough
9. I Don't Know What I Would Do Without You
10. I Let Go (Of Anything That Stops Me)
11. I'll Just Fall On You
12. I Love You, Holy Spirit
13. I'm Building My Life Around You
14. I'm Giving Myself To You
15. I'm In Love! I'm In Love!
16. I Need Water (Holy Spirit, You're My Well)

17. In The Secret Place
18. In Your Presence, I'm Always Changed
19. In Your Presence (Miracles Are Born)
20. I've Got To Live In Your Presence
21. I Want To Hear Your Voice
22. I Will Do Things Your Way
23. Just One Day At A Time
24. Meet Me In The Secret Place
25. More Than Ever Before
26. Nobody Else Does What You Do
27. No No Walls!
28. Nothing Else Matters Anymore (Since I've Been In The Presence Of You Lord)
29. Nowhere Else
30. Once Again You've Answered
31. Only A Fool Would Try (To Live Without You)

32. Take Me Now
33. Teach Me How To Please You
34. There's No Place I'd Rather Be
35. Thy Word Is All That Matters
36. When I Get In Your Presence
37. You're The Best Thing (That's Ever Happened To Me)
38. You Are Wonderful
39. You've Done It Once
40. You Keep Changing Me
41. You Satisfy

Add 10% For S/H

THE WISDOM CENTER
P.O. Box 99, Denton, Texas 76202

1-888-WISDOM1
(1-888-947-3661)

Website:
WWW.THEWISDOMCENTER.TV